Ariana Grande
The Ultimate Guide

Megan Stallwood

Contents

Introduction

Ariana Grande is an American singer, songwriter and actress.

At 30 years old she is one of the most successful and critically acclaimed music artists of all time and a pop culture icon. She is known for her wide vocal range. Ariana started off as a successful child actress with shows such as Victorious before starting her music career.

Ariana is popular on social media and an important cultural figure who espouses many charitable causes.

Find out more about Ariana's life and career with this book.

Ariana

Ariana was born on the 26th June 1993.

\-

Ariana was born in Boca Raton in Florida, USA. Boca Raton is located on the south eastern coast of Florida. The population is about 96000.

\-

Arianna's hair is actually curly.

\-

Ariana's family come from Sicily and Abruzzo in Italy.

\-

Ariana's favourite subject at school was science.

\-

In 2020 Ariana and Lady Gaga's Rain On Me

single replaced Ariana's Stuck With U at
Number One in the UK charts.

-

The money made from Ariana and Justin
Bieber's Stuck With U single in 2020 went to
the First Responders Children's Foundation
Charity.

-

Ariana is a vegan - she has a meat, fish and
dairy free diet.

-

Ariana wears glasses and contact lenses.

-

Although Ariana had acting roles when she
was younger - such as in Victorious - she says
she much preferred singing to acting.

-

Gloria Estefan is one of Ariana's favourite
singers.

She first saw the Cuban American Estefan on a

cruise ship when she was 8 years old.

-

When Ariana decided to become a singer she had received no singing training.

-

Ariana is is hypoglycemic. Hypoglycemia is a condition in which your blood sugar (glucose) level is lower than normal.

-

In 2019 Ariana headlined the famous Coachella Music Festival held at the Empire Polo Club in Indio, California located in the Coachella Valley in the Colorado Desert.

She became the fourth female artist to headline the festival after Beyoncé, Lady Gaga and Björk.

She was paid $8 million.

-

Classic FM wrote of Ariana :

'She has one of the most impressive ranges of

any female singer in the pop music industry
and she makes it all look So Darn Easy.'

-

Ariana is 5ft/1.52 metres tall.

-

Ariana has a 4 octave vocal range. The
average is 2 and 4 is rare.

-

Ariana says she is scared of the dark.

-

When not performing Ariana says she dresses
"very normally".

-

Ariana said this about her mother Joan:

"My mom is a CEO and owns a company that
manufactures communications equipment for
the Marines and the Navy, so she's not really
the housewife type, if you get what I'm
saying. She's the most badass, independent
woman you'll ever meet—not the cookies-in-

the-oven type."

-

Ariana did not manage to get into her school choir.

-

Ariana is a big fan of Rihanna and listens to her songs regularly. Her favourite rapper is Big Sean.

-

Ariana's favourite horror film is Nightmare on Elm Street (1984).

-

Ariana has over 50 tattoos.

-

Ariana's favourite karaoke songs is Lady Marmalade.

-

Ariana's Dangerous Woman tour grossed $71 million in just seven months.

Ariana said this of making her debut album Yours Truly in 2013:

"When I was making the album, I would start [filming] Sam & Cat at 6.30 in the morning and finish at 8.30[pm], then go to the studio till midnight and get home at 1am."

-

Ariana enjoys the Halloween time and wishes it could be Halloween every day.

-

The video for Thank U, Next had 55.4 million views on Youtube in the first 24 hours after being uploaded.

-

Ariana is a big fan of roller coaster. She is a fan of the Guardians of the Galaxy at Disney land.

-

Before Ariana became famous she had a Youtube channel where she would sing cover versions of songs.

-

Ariana disagrees that she is a diva and suggest she is just trying to express her opinions and have some control over her work.

"The word diva gets thrown around when someone is successful in all the wrong connotations. It gets completely misconstrued. It's an insult to a strong female energy. That diva energy really is about taking control. That's what I love about that word."

-

Ariana's favourite city is Paris in France.

-

Ariana has said that one superpower she would like is to be able to fly.

-

Ariana's first album took three years to make and Ariana says her voice changed and matured during the process.

-

One frustration Ariana has is that she is often misquoted in interviews.

-

Ariana earns about $50,000 per day from merchandise.

-

Ariana's favourite song by One Direction is One Thing.

-

Ariana started her Twitter account when she was 15.

-

Ariana has stated:

"I'm a huge advocate of self-expression, being yourself, and encouraging people to embrace who they are and the things that make them beautiful.

I love people's uniqueness—the quirky, weird, interesting, and different things about everybody."

-

Ariana's Honeymoon Tour in 2015 made $41.8 million.

-

Ariana's favourite perfumes?

Viktor & Rolf Flowerbomb, Trish McEvoy Sexy No. 9 Blackberry and Vanilla one and Givenchy Hot Couture.

-

Ariana's lucky number is 8.

-

As a child Ariana enjoyed singing along to the Wizard of Oz soundtrack.

-

Ariana has said:

"I would rather sell fewer records and be outspoken".

-

Ariana said of selfies:

"Everybody makes up these ridiculous captions
for their selfies that have nothing to do with
the picture, like 'Layin' in bed on Saturday.'
It's like, No, you are not! You just spent an
hour getting ready for this picture!

We all post a selfie for the same reason—
because we feel better about ourselves than
usual. So just be like, 'Hey, I feel good about
myself today, so here's a picture!'"

-

Ariana stated:

"You should feel grateful and happy that
you're healthy, you're alive, and that you are
loved.

Whatever weight you are, whatever situation
you're in, whether you have a breakout,
whatever it is—you are loved."

-

Republic Records signed Ariana after watching
her sing on her YouTube channel.

-

Ariana dabbled with the French horn as a child.

-

Ariana's advice for anyone who wants to act or sing:

"All I have to say is basically if performing, singing, acting and dancing is what you want to do, then you just have to do it—no matter where it is.

If there's a community theater, if there's a family theater, if there's just a little orchestra that you can sing with in your community or a school play, you have to keep performing no matter where it is, even if it's in your living room for your grandparents."

-

Ariana is a millennial – born between born between 1981 and 1996).

-

Ariana enjoys astronomy.

-

Ariana has confessed that on many occasions
her lyrics are not sung very clearly.

-

Ariana said:

"I'm not like a crazy girl in any way. Even if I
was just in high school, the furthest thing from
myself, I would never even go to a party. I'm
just a nerd.

I'm a big nerd. I love Harry Potter. I love
scary movies. I love dinosaurs, science, aliens,
ghosts."

-

Ariana has joked that her famous high ponytail
is like an "instant facelift"!

-

Ariana's emoji collection is called "Arimoji".

-

Ariana often wears oversized pullovers.

-

Ariana's favorite episode of Victorious is Survival of the Hottest.

-

Ariana said of being compared to Mariah Carey:

"If I complained about being compared to the greatest vocalist who ever lived, I would be a very dumb, ungrateful person. So I can't complain. It's a massive compliment."

-

Ariana said this on fashion:

"I don't really believe in any fashion rules. I think fashion is a form of self-expression, wear whatever you want."

Ariana encourages individuals to prioritize comfort and cuteness to exude their best selves.

-

Ariana's favourite lipstick? MAC Viva Glam.

-

2016's Dangerous Woman album was originally going to be titled Moonlight.

-

Ariana's song 7 Rings used the melody from the song My Favorite Things the Rodgers and Hammerstein song from the 1959 musical The Sound of Music. As a result 90% of the royalties from 7 Rings go to the rights owners of the original song.

-

Ariana is a fan of Imogen Heap especially her 2009 album Ellipse.

-

Ariana has had some Japanese language lessons for when she is in Japan.

Her Japanese language tutor says Ariana loves Japan because people are very petite there and so the fashions fit her.

-

Bloomberg called Ariana the "first pop diva of the streaming generation".

Ariana has brown eyes.

-

Ariana says she is amazed that her ponytail became so famous.

"Honestly, I wasn't expecting it to become a thing. I wasn't expecting to ever have a signature look. But it became one."

-

Ariana said that "Touch It" ranks as her least favorite among her songs, describing it as "boring."

-

Kourtney Kardashian dressed up as Ariana her for Halloween in 2018.

-

Ariana's fragrance sales reached an estimated $50 million in 2018.

-

Ariana is a big fan of Harry Potter and stated that she would love to marry Daniel Radcliffe!

Ariana wore a Harry Potter Wizards Chest Slytherin Headband on her Sweetener tour.

Ariana has the number the number 9¾ on her right-hand index finger

-

Ariana is a fan of rap and enjoys performing rap songs.

-

Ariana says she has nostalgic memories of the nineties.

"That was such a vivid time. I was obsessed with Missy Elliott, TLC and Eminem. Everything was so great. Nickelodeon had the best shows and the toys were dope and at P.E. time we had all the right things.

I was a '90s kid, but I was alive, I remember things. Cartoons were great, music was great."

-

Ariana became the 15th solo female artist to have her debut album top the Billboard 200 chart.

-

Ariana has said her stage persona is an exaggerated version of herself.

-

In December 2012 Ariana starred as Snow White in a musical version of the fairytale called A Snow White Christmas. The musical pantomime performed at the Pasdena Playhouse in California featured magic and famous songs by artists such as Britney Spears and Michael Jackson.

The show received positive reviews

-

Ariana is a dog lover and has several dogs.

-

Ariana and her mother have watched the Jersey Boys musical numerous times and are big fans.

This musical which was first staged in 2004 is about the Frankie Valli pop group The Four Seasons in the 1960s.

-

Ariana's cover of Mariah Carey's Emotions on her old YouTube channel during the had 33 million views.

-

Ariana said:

"And with all due respect to My Everything and Dangerous Woman, I feel like I played the game a lot on those two albums. I wanted to make dope records that would put me in a place where I could then make whatever I wanted. I kind of played the game a little bit."

-

In 2013, Ariana suffered vocal cord hemorrhage, forcing her to take a temporary break from singing.

-

Ariana is a fan of the singer and composer Lesley Gore.

Gore had a famous hit with It's My Party in 1963 and later composed songs for the film musical Fame in 1980.

-

Ariana has a birthmark on her left shoulder.

-

Ariana received the Young Influencer Award at the 2014 iHeart Radio Music Awards.

-

The debut of Victorious in 2010 marked the second-highest viewed debut in Nickelodeon's history.

-

A TikTok meme parodied Ariana's fondness for oversized sleeves and pullovers by depicting Ariana trying to wash her hands and getting her sleeves all wet.

-

During her childhood, Ariana predominantly listened to urban pop and '90s music.

-

All of Ariana's full-length albums have achieved platinum certification.

-

Ariana made her first television appearance as a child when she sang The Star-Spangled Banner for the Florida Panthers Ice Hockey Team in 2001 aged 8.

-

Ariana prefers coffee to tea.

\-

Although Ariana currently has limited interest in acting, she remains open to participating in a scary movie or a musical.

\-

Halloween holds a special place in Ariana's heart, as her family has always celebrated the holiday with a unique and quirky sense of humour.

\-

Ariana sold 2 million units of her debut single.

\-

Ariana follows a macrobiotic diet.

The term macrobiotics refers to a holistic lifestyle of eating and living in harmony with nature to promote a long, healthy life.

The main foods in a macrobiotic diet are whole grains, locally grown fresh veggies, sea veggies, and beans. You can also eat fruits, nuts, and seeds. You don't eat meat or dairy.

\-

Aurora is Ariana's favorite Disney Princess.

"I like Aurora, Sleeping Beauty, because she's just sleeping and looking pretty and waiting for boys to come kiss her. Sounds like a good life—lots of naps and cute boys fighting dragons to come kiss you."

-

If stranded on a desert island, Ariana's luxury items of choice would be her dogs, some books, and plenty of water.

-

In 2019, Ariana earned 22 Billboard Music Award nominations.

-

Ariana enjoys elliptical workouts on a machine accompanied by music.

-

No Tears Left To Cry achieved 3x Platinum certification in the US.

-

Ariana claims to have had supernatural experiences, including unsettling visions and encounters with unexplained phenomena.

Ariana believes she had a supernatural encounter at Stull Cemetery in Kansas City:

 "I felt this sick, overwhelming feeling of negativity over the whole car and we smelled sulfur, which is the sign of a demon, and there was a fly in the car randomly, which is another sign of a demon. I was like, 'This is scary, let's leave.'

I rolled down the window before we left and said, 'We apologize. We didn't mean to disrupt your peace.' Then I took a picture and there are three super distinct faces in the picture—they're faces of textbook demons."

-

Rain On Me achieved significant success with 8.1 million plays in seven days in Britain, marking the biggest-ever opening week for streaming numbers by an all-female collaboration in the UK.

-

Ariana is one of the ten most streamed artists

in Spotify history.

-

Ariana's first single Put Your Hearts Up was released in December 2011.

-

Ariana Grande is only the second woman in the history of the Hot 100 to debut three songs at number one. The first person to achieve this feat was Mariah Carey.

-

Ariana said that it hadn't been easy as a

teenager in the entertainment industry:

"I went right from middle school, like regular, everyday school, to Broadway. And that was a really crazy transition to make because it was so much hard work. I was like yay, no more school! Then I was like oh my God, I have to kill myself everyday dancing for more than 12 hours and sit on my couch everyday with Icy Hot and Tiger Balm and the whole house smelling like menthol and just waiting for my muscle pain to go away.

It's a lot of hard work and it's a lot of adjusting, but I'm learning so much, so I'm happy."

-

Ariana recalls an early audition:

"I had this one audition for a Broadway show. They did the dancing first, and I was all ready to dance and I was so excited. And I was really thrilled because I had done all the choreography correctly and I was like, 'Thank, God. I'm so, so, so excited.'

And they were cutting people straight from the audition and they said, 'You have to go because you weren't silly enough.' And I was like, 'What?' And they were like, 'You were supposed to make goofy faces.' And I was like, 'Excuse me?' And then that was it.

-

Ariana said on her Instagram layout:

 "I love making my Instagram look cohesive—look like a Tumblr page almost. When they all make sense colorwise, or when you add those white borders to them, it makes them look cleaner. Clean and precise."

-

Ariana said:

"Dancing in high heels is kind of tough. I learn the dances without the heels, and then we add them. We just practice, and I get used to it. My feet hurt really badly at the end of the shows, but it's fun. While it's happening it's fun. I feel tall."

-

Teen Vogue ranked Santa Tell Me as Ariana's best Christmas song.

-

Ariana says that she meditates every day.

-

Ariana has said that Jennifer Garner is one of her favourite actresses.

The 2004 Jennifer Garner comedy 13 Going On 30 is one of Ariana's favorite films.

The music video for Thank U, Next references the film 13 Going on 30.

-

Ariana's name came from Princess Oriana in the 1988 Felix the Cat movie.

-

Ariana did not want to do the ice bucket challenge and instead just made a donation to charity.

-

Ariana drinks coconut water which is considered to be extremely healthy.

She also uses coconut oil on her hair.

Ariana appears in the first season of horror tv series Scream Queens in 2015. She said she could not scream for real in the series as she had to look after her voice.

-

Ariana enjoys playing the board game Monopoly. She enjoys other board games as well, but often cannot find anyone to play as many people do not have the patience to play them.

-

The Dangerous woman tour sold 875,000 tickets.

-

Yours Truly went to number one on the iTunes Store charts in over 30 countries.

-

Ariana thinks the worst song on her album Thank U, Next is NASA.

-

In 2019 Forbes rated Ariana as the 62nd highest celebrity in the world.

-

Ariana's shoe size is 6.

-

Ariana's star sign is Cancer. Those of this zodiac sign are primarily known for being emotional, nurturing, and highly intuitive, as well as sensitive and at times insecure.

-

Ariana did not like her debut single Put Your Hearts Up released in December 2011:

"It was geared toward kids and felt so inauthentic and fake. For the video, they gave me a bad spray tan and put me in a princess dress and had me frolic around the street. The whole thing was straight out of hell. I still have nightmares about it.

Sonically it's just not my vibe. I think it would've been a great hit song for somebody else maybe, but it's just not what I like to sing. It's a bubblegum pop record for sure, and I like to sing stuff that's a little more soulful. I love pop music, I'm a huge pop music fan, but I just didn't think that that record was right for me."

-

Ariana had Put Your Hearts Up removed from her Vevo page as soon as she could.

-

Ariana works with celebrity trainer Harley Pasternak.

Harley also works with celebrities such Rihanna, Ladt Gaga and Robert Downey Jr.

-

Ariana posted some makeup free selfies in 2020 which showed some rarely seen freckles.

-

Teen Vogue ranked the 2019 Monopoly by Ariana and Victoria Monétas one of the best prom songs.

-

Ariana has a tattoo of a heart behind her ear.

-

Ariana said that she would like to produce music for other artists in the future:

"I would love to do that. Not yet, because I want to focus on my music for that but yeah."

-

Ariana says her favorite word is bubble.

-

Ariana has a hand tattoo of BABYDOLL. This is a family nickname for her.

-

Shoe designer Giuseppe Zanotti was much impressed by Ariana's ability to dance in high shoes:

"Musicians and dancers usually require chunkier and lower heels to feel more secure on stage. Ariana is one of the only talents to perform with ease in skyscraper platforms. Ariana loves very high platforms and over-the-knee boots. For the (Sweetener) tour, she specifically requested full-length durable zippers to allow easy changes between performances."

-

Ariana is a fan of the singer Brandy.

-

Ariana says she has a weakness for comedians and funny awkward men:

"I love funny guys! I love silly, funny awkward boys. I love boys who can make fools of themselves and don't take themselves too seriously."

-

Ariana is the most followed woman on Instagram but has confessed she does not know how the site works.

-

Ariana says she sleeps in a king size bed so that her dogs have the option of jumping on.

-

Ariana recorded an operatic duet with Andrea Bocelli in 2015 called E Píu Ti Penso.

-

Ariana says she has never liked going to the gym.

-

In 2019, Ariana entered Forbes' annual list of the world's 100 highest-paid celebrities.

-

Ariana's 2013 song Honeymoon Avenue is one of her favourites.

-

In February 2019, Ariana had the number-one, number-two, and number-three songs in America. Only The Beatles had ever done this before.

-

Ariana enjoys ice skating.

-

Ariana has had her own line with fashion retailer Lipsy London.

-

It took forty minutes to paint Ariana's body with waterproof paint for the God is a Woman video.

-

In 2019, Ariana became the face of fashion house Givenchy:

"Givenchy is a house I have forever admired," said Ariana. "I love this clothing and the confidence and joy it brings to the people wearing it. Not only is the clothing timeless and beautiful but I'm proud to work with a brand that makes people feel celebrated for who they are, and unapologetic about whatever they want to be."

-

In 2019, Ariana transformed her home into a haunted house for a Halloween party. The guests included Lizzo, Nicki Minaj, and Demi Lovato.

-

Ariana speaks some Spanish and would like to record Spanish language songs in the future.

\-

Ariana says she has a great fear of being disliked.

\-

Ariana's Manhattan apartment has a private IMAX theater.

\-

Ariana is a fan of 80s sitcom The Golden Girls.

\-

Ariana had her handprints put in cement at Planet Hollywood in New York on December 22 2011.

\-

Makeup artist Ashley K Holm explained Ariana's unique eye-makeup look:

"Use an angled eyeliner brush to extend the wing, and make sure the wing is angled upward towards the tail end of your eyebrows to lift the eyes up."

-

Ariana is a big fan of 1950s fashions.

-

Ariana says she can't whistle.

-

Ariana said:

"Love is a really scary thing, and you never know what's going to happen. It's one of the most beautiful things in life, but it's one of the most terrifying. It's worth the fear because you have more knowledge, experience, you learn from people, and you have memories."

-

Discover Music said of Dangerous Woman :

"For her third studio album, Grande would stage one of her greatest reinventions. At this point in her career, some still questioned the maturity of Grande's music. With its sleek sensuality and vocalese delivery, Dangerous Woman not only served as a barbed rejoinder to her critics but introduced a new side to Grande as a confident young woman i."

-

Stylist to the stars Chris Appleto says that Ariana uses Gorilla Snot Gel. "It's called Gorilla Snot. It's a gel. Say I wanted to do a ponytail and I wanted to do something really slick, I'd just put that on the edges. It makes it like rock solid."

-

Ariana passed her driving test in 2012.

\-

Ariana had to cancel two concerts in Florida in 2018 because she was suffering from a tomato allergy.

\-

Ariana prefers the left side of her face to be prominent in photographs although studies have shown there is no difference between the two sides of her face.

Ariana has said she dislikes looking straight into the camera lens:

"I see people on the other side of the lens and the whole judgmental world of pop culture waiting with their pitchforks and torches. At the end of the day I don't care what they have to say, but knowing that every little thing I do is documented is a lot of pressure. I guess that's where it comes from."

\-

In the United States, the name Ariana peaked as the 37th most popular name for baby girls in 2014

-

The video for Break free is a sci-fi homage that riffs on Star Trek, Flash Gordon, Forbidden Planet, Star Trek, Planet of the Apes, and other songs.

-

Ariana likes Grether's Pastilles; many singers use Grether's Pastilles because they don't contain menthol which dries up the throat.

-

Ariana thinks her fashion is a blend of Marilyn Monroe and Audrey Hepburn.

-

Ariana's first three albums were quickly certified platinum by the RIAA.

-

During the 2020 quarantine, Ariana ruled out releasing a new album. "I don't really feel comfortable putting anything out right now. Because other than this [Stuck With U], it's a really tricky time for all of that.

Ariana said - "If I'm going to be a role model, the last thing I should be is perfect because that's not realistic. As long as I'm honest and genuine and I share with my fans my truest self, that's the best that I can do because that's allowing them to do the same thing."

-

Ariana said her dream dinner party guests would be Imogen Heap, her grandmother, Leonardo DiCaprio, Michael Jackson, and Audrey Hepburn.

-

Ariana wore a pair of Lorraine Schwartz emerald and diamond earrings at the 2020 Grammy awards.

She said:

"Those earrings, they are sorely and deeply missed. I think of them constantly and wish we didn't have to part."

-

LeRoy Bennett, Ariana's creative director and tour production designer, said - "She's very black and white. She's either absolutely over the moon, loves something, or she really hates it. So you always know where you stand with her."

-

Ariana has a hilltop mansion in Beverly Hills.

-

Ariana has said - "I often thought that I would love to be a graphic designer."

-

On her makeup routine, Ariana said:

"I don't use a lot of powder, so I don't ever get powder in my lashes."

-

Ariana has been seen in glasses but prefers contact lenses

-

Ariana said of her stage dancing:

"There's a lot of strutting to the beat. There's

a lot of sitting down and leg-kicking and voguing and posing and hair flipping involved."

-

The set for the Sweetener tour was inflatable.

-

Ariana prefers walking in the hills near her home than going to the gym.

-

Ariana dislikes sunshine and hot weather:

 "I'm like, please bring me the cold and the clammy and the clouds. You want what you didn't grow up getting."

Ariana frequently posts pictures of her meals on Instagram.

-

Ariana does not mention most of her tattoos. Many of them are hidden very well.

-

Victoria Monet and British girl group Little Mix

opened for Ariana at some shows in 2016.

-

The ARIANA GRANDE THANK, U NEXT
fragrance was marketed as:

'A fragrance that is inspired by Ariana
Grande's hit and anthem song, Thank U, Next.
It has top notes of white pear and wild
raspberry; heart notes of crème de coconut
and pink rose petals; and a dry down of
macaroon sugar and velvet musk.'

-

Billie Eilish said that Ariana has given her
advice on how to cope with the pressures of
fame

-

In 2021 Ariana appeared in Netflix movie
Don't Look Up, alongside Leonardo DiCaprio,
Jennifer Lawrence, and Meryl Streep. The film
is about a comet falling on Earth. It had record
views and gained positive reviews.

-

In 2023 Ariana released a reissue of her debut

studio album, Yours Truly (Tenth Anniversary Edition).

-

Ariana's Youtube channel has over 50 million subscribers and has had 24 billion views.

Discography

Albums

Yours Truly

August 30, 2013

My Everything

August 22, 2014

Dangerous Woman

May 20, 2016

Sweetener

August 17, 2018

Thank U, Next

February 8, 2019

Positions

October 30, 2020

Live albums

Compilation albums

The Remix

May 25, 2015 (in Japan)

The Best

September 27, 2017

Extended plays

Christmas Kisses

December 13, 2013

Christmas & Chill

December 18, 2015

Singles

As lead artist

Put Your Hearts Up
(2011)

The Way (featuring Mac Miller)
(2013)

Baby I
(2013)

Right There (featuring Big Sean)
(2013)

Problem(featuring Iggy Azalea)
(2014)

Break Free (featuring Zedd)
(2014)

Bang Bang (with Jessie J and Nicki Minaj)
(2014)

Love Me Harder (with the Weeknd)
(2014)

One Last Time
(2015)

Focus
(2015)

Dangerous Woman
(2016)

Into You
(2016)

Side to Side (featuring Nicki Minaj)
(2016)

Everyday (featuring Future)
(2017)

Beauty and the Beast (with John Legend)
(2017)

No Tears Left to Cry
(2018)

God Is a Woman
(2018)

Breathin
(2018)

Thank U, Next
(2018)

7 Rings

(2019)

Break Up with Your Girlfriend, I'm
Bored
(2019)

Boyfriend (with Social House)
(2019)

Don't Call Me Angel (with Miley Cyrus and
Lana Del Rey)
(2019)

Stuck with U (with Justin Bieber)
(2020)

Rain on Me (with Lady Gaga)
(2020)

Positions
(2020)

34+35 (solo or remix featuring Doja Cat and
Megan Thee Stallion)
(2020)

POV
(2021)

Save Your Tears (remix) (with the Weeknd)
(2021)

Die for You (remix) (with the Weeknd)
(2023)

As featured artist

Popular Song (Mika featuring Ariana Grande)
(2012)

Adore (Cashmere Cat featuring Ariana Grande)
(2015)

Boys Like You (Who Is Fancy featuring Meghan
Trainor and Ariana Grande)
(2015)

Over and Over Again (Nathan Sykes featuring
Ariana Grande)
(2016)

My Favorite Part (Mac Miller featuring Ariana
Grande)
(2016)

Faith (Stevie Wonder featuring Ariana Grande)
(2016)

Heatstroke (Calvin Harris featuring Young
Thug, Pharrell Williams and Ariana Grande
(2017)

Quit (Cashmere Cat featuring Ariana Grande)
(2017)

Dance to This (Troye Sivan featuring Ariana Grande)
(2018)

Bed (Nicki Minaj featuring Ariana Grande)
(2018)

Rule the World (2 Chainz featuring Ariana Grande)
(2019)

Good as Hell (Remix; Lizzo featuring Ariana Grande)
(2019)

Time (Childish Gambino featuring Ariana Grande)
(2020)

Met Him Last Night (Demi Lovato featuring Ariana Grande)
(2021)

Christmas/Holiday Singles

Last Christmas
(2013)

Love Is Everything
(2013)

Snow in California
(2013)

Santa Baby (featuring Liz Gillies)
(2013)

Santa Tell Me
(2014)

A Hand for Mrs. Claus (with Idina Menzel)
(2019)

Oh Santa! (Mariah Carey featuring Ariana Grande and Jennifer Hudson)
(2020)

It Was a... (Masked Christmas) (Jimmy Fallon featuring Ariana Grande and Megan Thee Stallion)
(2021)

Santa, Can't You Hear Me (with Kelly Clarkson)
(2022)

Promotional singles

L.A. Boyz (Victorious cast featuring Victoria
Justice and Ariana Grande)
2012)

Almost Is Never Enough (with Nathan Sykes)
(2013)

Best Mistake (featuring Big Sean)
(2014)

Brand New You (featuring Brynn Williams and
Caitlin Gann)
(2014)

This Is Not a Feminist Song (Saturday Night
Live cast featuring Ariana Grande)
(2016)

Be Alright
(2016)

Let Me Love You (featuring Lil Wayne)
(2016)

Jason's Song (Gave It Away)
(2016)

Somewhere Over the Rainbow
(2017)

Arturo Sandoval (Arturo Sandoval and Pharrell Williams featuring Ariana Grande)
(2018)

The Light Is Coming (featuring Nicki Minaj)
(2018)

Imagine
(2018)

Monopoly (with Victoria Monét)
(2019)

Just Look Up (with Kid Cudi)
(2021)

Other Charted Songs

Give It Up (Victorious cast featuring Elizabeth Gillies and Ariana Grande)
(2011)

Honeymoon Avenue
(2013)

Tattooed Heart
(2013)

Daydreamin
(2013)

You'll Never Know
(2013)

Break Your Heart Right Back (featuring
Childish Gambino)
(2014)

Break Your Heart Right Back (featuring
Childish Gambino)
(2014)

My Everything
(2014)

All My Love (Major Lazer featuring Ariana
Grande)
(2014)

Get On Your Knees (Nicki Minaj featuring
Ariana Grande)
(2014)

Wit It This Christmas
(2015)

December
(2015)

True Love
(2015)

Winter Things
(2015)

Moonlight
(2016)

Greedy
(2016)

Leave Me Lonely (featuring Macy Gray)
(2016)

Bad Decisions
(2016)

Touch It
(2016)

Thinking Bout You
(2016)

Raindrops (An Angel Cried)
(2018)

Blazed (featuring Pharrell Williams)
(2018)

R.E.M
(2018)

Sweetener
(2018)

Successful
(2018)

Everytime
(2018)

Borderline
(featuring Missy Elliott)
(2018)

Better Off
(2018)

Goodnight n Go
(2018)

Pete Davidson
(2018)

Get Well Soon
(2018)

Needy
(2019)

NASA
(2019)

Bloodline
(2019)

Fake Smile
(2019)

Bad Idea
(2019)

Make Up
(2019)

Ghostin
(2019)

In My Head
(2019)

Bad to You (with Normani and Nicki Minaj)
(2019)

Nobody (with Chaka Khan)
(2019)

How I Look on You
(2019)

Got Her Own (with Victoria Monét)
(2019)

Shut Up
(2020)

Motive (with Doja Cat)
(2020)

Just like Magic
(2020)

Off the Table (with the Weeknd)
(2020)

Six Thirty
(2020)

Safety Net(featuring Ty Dolla Sign)
(2020)

My Hair
(2020)

Nasty
(2020)

West Side
(2020)

Love Language
(2020)

Obvious
(2020)

Someone like U
(2021)

Test Drive
(2021)

Worst Behavior
(2021)

Main Thing
(2021)

I Don't Do Drugs (Doja Cat featuring Ariana
Grande)
(2021)

Honeymoon Avenue(live from London)
(2023)

The Way (live from London; featuring Mac
Miller)
(2023)

Ariana Recipes

Ariana has a penchant for strawberries, indulging in them on most days. Given her hypoglycemic condition, she ensures she keeps a chocolate or protein bar handy to prevent her blood sugar levels from dropping when she forgets to eat.

Expressing her love for baking, Ariana typically starts her day with oatmeal or a refreshing fruit smoothie. Her palate extends to diverse foods, including daikon, lotus root, and a variety of fruits such as dates, strawberries, raspberries, blueberries, and dragon fruit.

Ariana also appreciates aszuki beans, edamame, and a selection of vegetables like broccoli, carrots, potatoes, and sweet potatoes. Cashew nuts find a place among her favorites, reflecting her diverse taste.

Despite her Italian heritage, Ariana, who follows a vegan diet, rarely indulges in Italian cuisine due to its meat and cheese-centric nature. However, pasta remains an exception.

In pursuit of health benefits, Ariana includes coconut water and dandelion tea in her beverage choices. She has a liking for cinnamon, cayenne, and spinach, and takes pleasure in cultivating lemons in her backyard.

A unique culinary preference of Ariana involves dipping French fries in chocolate spread. She has a particular fondness for protein bars, favoring brands like Think Thin, Live Raw, and Pure. Pastilles, especially Grether's Pastilles, are her go-to for throat health.

Avocados, soy green lattes, strawberry kombucha tea, blackberries, and watermelon-mint juice also feature on Ariana's list of favored foods and beverages. Tofu constitutes a substantial part of her meals, and chocolate emerges as her preferred ice cream flavor.

Ariana relishes grilled vegetables, black bean spaghetti, pineapple, Trader Joe's Nut & Berry mix, and baked squash seeds. Popcorn, especially the Skinny Pop brand with various flavors, is another snack she enjoys.

A preference for gluten-free ice cream, noodles, seaweed, and Razzles (an American candy) adds to the diversity of Ariana's culinary interests. She appreciates teriyaki sauce, green beans, guava juice, bell peppers, and butternut squash, particularly in noodle form.

Embracing vegan sushi, Ariana displays a love for garlic, coffee over tea, and a taste for miso in her dishes. She has transitioned to a healthier diet, incorporating whole grains such as brown rice, barley, millet, and oats.

Ariana's breakfast of choice often includes whole oats with almond milk, topped with blueberries and almonds, as revealed in a Snapchat share. Her trainer, Harley Pasternak, notes her fondness for Japanese food, highlighting dishes like sea vegetable hijiki, edamame, daikon, and a vegan version of the Japanese pancake okonomiyaki.

Lastly, Ariana's 25th birthday party featured a 40-pound piñata cake filled with rainbow candy and sprinkles, underscoring her sweet tooth. Her eclectic tastes extend to artichoke dip, chocolate almond milk, kale, and iced coffee with non-dairy milk.

Here are a selection of Ariana's favourite recipes.

Lime Popcorn

Ingredients

450g/2 cups of popcorn kernels
2 tablespoons of oil
lime juice

Put the oil in a saucepan. When hot add the popcorn. Cover. Cook until popcorn is made.

Vegan Sushi

Ingredients

Nori sheets
cooked sushi rice
sliced shitake mushrooms
cucumber slices
chopped bell pepper
chopped avocado
grated carrot
soy sauce
rice vinegar
sugar
sea salt

Coat the mushrooms in some soy sauce and cook in a preheated oven at 204C/400F for 20 minutes.

Mix 4 tablespoons of rice vinegar, 2 tablespoons of sugar and 2 teaspoons of sea salt in a pan. Cook on a medium heat for 8 minutes until the sugar has dissolved.

Add mix to 200g/8 cups of rice.

Spread rice on the nori sheets. Add vegetable pieces of your choice. Then roll the nori to make the sushi roll.

Dip into soy sauce.

Okonomiyaki Pancake

Ingredients

100g/3.5 oz of chopped lotus root
half a mashed ripe banana
1 chopped scallion/spring onion
half a peeled and grated potato
half a shredded cabbage
1 tablespoon of grated ginger
100g/3.5 oz of flour
1 teaspoon of soy sauce
100ml/3.3 fl oz of vegetable stock
salt
pepper

Mix the flour, banana and stock. Make as smooth mix. Add the potato and some salt and pepper. Leave for 1 hour.

Add the cabbage, ginger, scallion, soy and lotus root to the mix. stir.

Put some oil in a pan. Add a thin layer to the pan and fry for 4 minutes on each side.

Butternut Squash Noodles

Ingredients

noodles from 1 butternut squash or prepared
butternut squash noodles
1 chopped bell pepper
240g/1 cup chopped tofu
4 chopped button mushrooms
100ml/3.3 fl oz almond milk (non sweetened)
2 tablespoons nutritional yeast
half a tablespoon of arrowroot
salt
pepper
olive oil

Cook the noodles in some olive oil for 4
minutes. Add the mushrooms, tofu and bell
pepper and cook for 7 minutes. Add some salt
and pepper.

Mix the milk, arrowroot and yeast. Add to the
mix. Cook on a medium heat for 7 minutes,
until thickened. Add some salt and pepper.

Acai Bowl with Blackberries

Ingredients

2 teaspoons of acai powder
5 strawberries
3 tablespoons of frozen blackberries
3 tablespoons of chopped pineapple
1 teaspoon of flaked coconut
3 tablespoons of ice cubes
water

Put the acai, blackberries, strawberries and ice cubes in a blender. Add 130ml/4.3 fl oz of water. Blend until smooth. Top with pineapple and coconut flakes to serve.

Vegan Nutella

Ingredients

520g/4 cups of unsalted roasted hazelnuts
1 teaspoon of sea salt
140g/1 cup of vegan chocolate
1 teaspoon of vanilla extract
2 teaspoons of maple syrup

Remove skin from nuts.

Blend the nuts to make a butter type mix.

Melt the chocolate. Add the chocolate, maple syrup, salt and vanilla extract to the nuts and mix.

Can be stored for up to three weeks.

Green Tea Latte

Ingredients

240ml/1 cup of soy milk
1 tablespoons of matcha (green tea powder)
2 tablespoons of sugar
240ml/1 cup of water

Put the ingredients in a pan. Cook on a medium heat stirring constantly for 8 minutes. Serve in cups.

Cupcakes

Ingredients

160ml/5.4 fl oz of almond milk
1 tablespoon of Arrowroot mixed with 1
tablespoon of water
100g/3.5 oz of vegan margarine/spread
100g/3.5 oz of caster sugar
100g/3.5 oz of flour
1 teaspoon of vanilla extract

for topping

100g/3.5 oz of vegan margarine/spread
200g/7 oz of icing sugar
1 teaspoon of vanilla extract
2 drops of food colouring (vegan)

Mix sugar and margarine. Add vanilla,
arrowroot and almond milk, then gradually
add the flour. Make a smooth mix. Pour into
cupcake moulds/cups then cook at 180C/356F
for 25 minutes.

Mix the topping ingredients to make a paste.
Put on top of cooled cupcakes.

Ariana Quiz

1.
What was Ariana's favourite subject at school?

A. Math
B. Geography
C. Musician
D. Science

2.
Where are Ariana's family from?

A. Norway
B. Mexico
C. Italy
D. Slovakia

3.
What is the name of Ariana's brother?

A. Frankie
B. Terry
C. Gustavo
D. Michael

4.
How tall is Ariana?

A. 4ft 1/1.24 m
B. 5 ft/1.52 M
C. 5.3 ft/1.61 cm
D. 4.6 ft/1.4 m

5.
which of these tattoos does Ariana not have?

A. Leaves on ribcage
B. Parrot on elbow
C. Pokémon character Eevee.
D. "Let's Sing" in Japanese.

6.
What colour are Ariana's eyes?

A. Blue
B. Green
C. Amber
D. Brown

7.
How many of Ariana's albums been certified platinum?

A. One
B. All
C. Three
D. Five

8.
Which one of these is not the name of one of Ariana's dogs

A. Lionel
B. Coco
C. Fawkes
D. Cinnamon

9.
What is Ariana's full name?

A. Ariana Grande
B. Betty Grande
C. Ariana Grande-Butera
D. Ariana Rogers-Grande

10.
Who did Ariana play in Victorious?

A. Victorious
B. Jade West
C. Trina Vega

D.Cat Valentine

11.
Who did Ariana perform Rain On Me with?

A. Mariah Carey
B. Lady Gaga
C. Nicki Minaj
D. Lana Del Ray

12.
In which year was Ariana's album Dangerous Woman released?

A. 2011
B.2020
C. 2014
D.2016

13.
What is Ariana's star sign?

A. Cancer
B. Leo
C. Aquarious
D. Aries

Answers to Quiz Questions:

1. D. Science

2. C. Italy

3. A. Frankie

4. B. 5 ft/1.52 M

5. B. Parrot on elbow

6. D. Brown

7. B. All

8. A. Lionel

9. C. Ariana Grande-Butera

10. D. Cat Valentine

11. B. Lady Gaga

12. D. 2016

13. A. Cancer

www.ingramcontent.com/pod-product-compliance
Lightning Source LLC
Chambersburg PA
CBHW031124160726

47989CB00016B/1396